A Trip to the
FARM
with SESAME STREET

Christy Peterson

Lerner Publications ◆ Minneapolis

Elmo and his friends from *Sesame Street* are going on a field trip, and you're invited! Field trips provide children with the opportunity to explore their communities, visit new places, and experience hands-on learning. This series brings the joys of field trips to your fingertips. Where will you go next?

—Sincerely, the Editors at Sesame Street

TABLE OF CONTENTS

FARM FIELD TRIP

Today we are visiting a farm! This farmer is going to show us her farm.

Some farms grow plants, and some raise animals.

Some farms do both.

4

This farmer has a big tractor. She uses the tractor to plant and harvest crops in the field.

Today the farmer is using a tractor to help plant seeds.

In the spring, farmers plant corn seeds. Then the corn is ready to pick from June to September.

Me love corn on the cob! Me help water plants.

In the summer, farmers pick blueberries off the bush and put them in bins.

11

In the fall, orange pumpkins are ready to harvest.

This farm has a flock of chickens. The chickens lay eggs for the farmer to sell.

Elmo gets to help feed the chickens.

Farmers bring the vegetables and fruits they've grown to the store or a farmer's market.

They bring eggs to the farmer's market too.

The farmer's market is full of yummy foods!

People from the community come to the store.
They buy fruits, vegetables, or eggs for their families.

19

Farms harvest crops and feed
communities all year round.
What is your favorite farm food?

FARM AT HOME!

You can grow food at home! Ask an adult for a pot, some soil, and seeds of your favorite fruit or vegetable. You could try growing **carrots**, **lettuce**, **tomatoes**, **berries**, or another crop! Put some soil into the pot. Then follow the directions on the seed packet.

- **Your seeds may need to be planted deeply. Or they may only need to be covered with a little soil.**

- **Some plants need lots of water or sunlight. Others don't need much of either.**

- **Check on your plant regularly, and watch it grow!**

GLOSSARY

abuela: grandmother in Spanish

community: people who live and work in an area

crop: a plant grown on a farm, especially a grain, fruit, or vegetable

flock: a group of animals on a farm, such as chickens or sheep

harvest: to pick, sort, and pack a crop

tractor: a vehicle with large rear wheels used to pull farm equipment

vegetable: a plant or part of a plant that people and animals eat

LEARN MORE

Carr, Aaron. *Tractors*. New York: AV2 by Weigl, 2022.

Harris, Bizzy. *Chickens on the Farm*. Minneapolis: Jump!, 2021.

Nelson, Robin. *The Story of Corn: It Starts with a Seed*. Minneapolis: Lerner Publications, 2021.

INDEX

PHOTO ACKNOWLEDGMENTS

Image credits: Ninja SS/Shutterstock.com, pp. 4–5; Fotokostic/Shutterstock.com, pp. 6–7; TDKvisuals/Shutterstock.com, p. 8; chanwangrong/Shutterstock.com, p. 9; Andersen Ross Photography Inc/DigitalVision/Getty Images, p. 10; kali9/E+/Getty Images, p. 12; JamesChen/Shutterstock.com, p. 13; mar_chm1982/Shutterstock.com, p. 14; Monkey Business Images/Shutterstock.com, pp. 16–17; Rawpixel.com/Shutterstock.com, p. 19; MNStudio/Shutterstock.com, p. 20.

Lerner Publications Company
An imprint of Lerner Publishing Group, Inc.
241 First Avenue North
Minneapolis, MN 55401 USA

For reading levels and more information, look up this title at www.lernerbooks.com.

Main body text set in Mikado a.
Typeface provided by HVD Fonts.

Editor: Andrea Nelson

Library of Congress Cataloging-in-Publication Data

Names: Peterson, Christy, author.
Title: A trip to the farm with Sesame Street / Christy Peterson.
Description: Minneapolis: Lerner Publications, [2022] | Series: Sesame Street field trips | Includes bibliographical references and index. | Audience: Ages 4–8 | Audience: Grades K–1 | Summary: "Join Elmo, Grover, and more friends from Sesame Street as they explore a farm and learn about the people who work there. Readers can try their hand at farming with a grow-your-own-food activity"—Provided by publisher.
Identifiers: LCCN 2021010397 (print) | LCCN 2021010398 (ebook) | ISBN 9781728439143 (library binding) | ISBN 9781728445052 (ebook)
Subjects: LCSH: Farms—Juvenile literature. | Farm life—Juvenile literature.
Classification: LCC S521 .P48 2022 (print) | LCC S521 (ebook) | DDC 630—dc23

LC record available at https://lccn.loc.gov/2021010397
LC ebook record available at https://lccn.loc.gov/2021010398

Manufactured in the United States of America
1-49820-49688-7/12/2021